MW01169094

Library of Congress Cataloging-in-Publication Data

Franklin, Ray
    On-The-Job Speech Training / Ray Franklin, 1st edition
    ISBN 978-0-615-21963-9
    1. Speech Training 2. Executives - speeches 3. Presentations

Printed in the United States of America

On-The-Job Speech Training

Public speaking tools to build on your professional success.

by Ray Franklin
The 8-minute speech coach

Available online from:
Stage America, LLC
702-259-7233
www.stageamerica.com
rfranklin@stageamerica.com

TABLE OF CONTENTS

- "You want me to speak to a large audience?"
- A very short history lesson
- My job – then and now
- How I fine-tuned this 8-minute coaching process

- "This is a football."
- Getting started
- Organization: the first tool in the box
- Create a one-sentence objective
- No more than 3 "thoughts to remember"
- Have you heard about the six-year-old who asked his mother, "Where did I come from?"
- Write a test script
- Don't begin production on slides, videos, etc, until the test script is complete
- Use less time than you're allotted
- Tell the audience what your message will be. Tell 'em your message. Tell 'em what you've told 'em.
- Include a call to action for your audience
- Ask for audience questions if time permits
- Say "thank you"
- Introduce the next person

Contents

Contents

- Beyond Bullet Points
- Is this too much on one slide?
- Screen size and placement
- Exit stage right?
- PowerPoint 3-ups
- Successful Q&A
- The audience-polling technology tool
- Panel discussions

- Teaching these tools to a willing participant
- And finally ...

ACKNOWLEDGEMENTS

I very much appreciate the work of Eileen Schwarz-Duty and Jeff Lightburn, who edited my speaking voice to become this useful written tool. Their efforts reinforce the knowledge that the written word and the spoken word have separate doctrines.

John Matz did a great job on the cover and illustrations. My hope was to keep them simple but illustrative. I hope you agree with our choices.

With clients like Hill & Knowlton, DuPont, GE Capital, Corinthian Colleges, Johnson & Johnson, Taco Bell, and Bank One for very long runs, I very much appreciate the opportunity to coach talented young people who discovered, after being hired, they would have to speak to large groups to advance their careers.

Production companies have included me on their team to focus on the presentation skills of their clients. I am very appreciative of those relationships.

My live event support team continues to execute their jobs so well that I have been able to master this subject. Thanks to Mike Benson, Jim and Eileen Duty, Harold Blumberg, Louis Mawcinitt, David Flad, Marc Wollin, John Matz and others.

Special thanks also to Linda Bjornson who continues to stay by my side through all this learning.

My hope is everyone who reads this book and applies the tools taught for so many years send me notes on how their careers were enhanced by what they learned here.

INTRODUCTION

"You want me to speak to a large audience?"

You never expected to be in this position. Your boss always does a great job at these meetings. Never in a million years did you anticipate having to stand up there as well. As a product manager or specialist with the firm, you are now charged with the responsibility to communicate your knowledge at the next meeting.

Delivering presentations to large groups was probably not on your resume, in your job description, or listed in the skills required for the job. It is now!

This is not a book on "How to Write" an effective speech, but rather, "How to Deliver" a knockout presentation with confidence.

We've all seen what happens when politicians, clergy, even co-workers stand before an audience and deliver a message that is interesting, informative, and welcomed by all.

We've also seen what happens when someone is ill-prepared and unsuccessfully attempts to deliver a message on stage.

You won't find an "easy" answer here, but you
will benefit from this book's proven "toolbox"
of successful speaking techniques. When used
and practiced, these "tools" will result in great
experiences as you speak in front of **any** audience.

A very short history lesson

First, a little background on me and how I came to
develop this proven method of helping people just
like you look and sound like the professionals they
are.

The business climate was quite different when I
started in the '70s as a production director of live
corporate events.

After college I worked in TV news. I was trained
"on-the-job" for studio and field news reporting
and interviewing. Whether I was at a small market
station in Miami or on network news in New York
or Washington, I had to be concerned about the
message and how it was delivered.

I traded my on-camera TV news job for what was
then called "Business Theater."

Corporate business meetings at the time were run
by the advertising agency. The meetings were slick
and well rehearsed. They used actors, singers, and
dancers, custom music, and theatrical effects.

The show often came to a screeching halt when the company executive would deliver his obligatory two-minute segment while glued to a lectern or teleprompter.

Then the slick production would continue with pyrotechnics and magic.

It was not unusual for a new-car dealer meeting to cost $5 to $8 million. The production costs for new product announcements, employee or distributor motivation continued to escalate until companies realized they needed to get a better return on their production investment.

Substance became more important than hoopla.

These days, there are fewer Broadway-style singing and dancing numbers at corporate events. Budgets are limited.

This transformation has caused companies to look internally for their own people to deliver a quality message.

As a result, people within the firm don't have the time or the budget to support lavish productions, and so they must rely on PowerPoint graphics created either internally or with a production company.

Perhaps you are one of those now required
to present a narrow message to an internal
or external audience. People still complain
about how much time it takes. "I can't do that
because I have a real job." Get used to it: giving
presentations is now a part of your "real job."

My job – then and now

Technically, my job is to deliver the equipment
and the personnel to make the meeting happen
with perfection. But for every business meeting
I am hired to direct, I consider my first job to be
audience advocate, although it is never described
that way.

Looking at presentations from the audience's
perspective' it was clear most corporate speakers
needed on-the-job coaching for success on the
platform.

The better corporate meetings have off-site
rehearsals, usually in a training or meeting room
at Headquarters. It is easy to see the first-timers.
They stammer; they don't know what to do with
their hands; and they wander around the stage
area constantly fixated on their notes.

Without some intervention the message would
not be delivered, the audience would not benefit,
and the first-timer would be judged for his or her
performance rather than the material.

I began to intervene, coaching market managers, product specialists, and junior account executives forced to speak, to ensure their success.

Proof of my success was a very personal letter I received from a junior marketing manager for a pharmaceutical company when he was promoted to VP of marketing after only four years with the company. He told me that he had three sources to thank for being where he was today: his God, his mother, and me his speech coach.

In 1979, that was pretty impressive. Since then, I've gathered hundreds of similar success stories and letters of appreciation illustrating how being a strong speaker directly related their rise up the corporate ladder and their ability to stand and deliver.

How I fine-tuned this 8-minute coaching process

For many years, GE Capital – the financial arm of GE – held its annual leadership meeting for their 600 top people in Puerto Rico. At the time, GE was headed by CEO Jack Welch and President of GE Capital Gary Wendt. Welch and Wendt insisted on excellence in all aspects of business, starting with people excellence. The two company leaders insisted their employees constantly improve their skills.

Throughout this period, GE Capital was the global leader in finance while delivering double-digit growth year, after year, after year. Sitting in the audience in Puerto Rico each year was the best of the best.

Every year during my nine-year association with GE, I worked with 60 to 70 people from around the world who had been selected to give a 3 to 5 minute presentation to this audience on their particular business specialty.

It was not unusual for someone to be selected to make their presentation less than a week before the meeting in Puerto Rico.

Needless to say, the pressure on those speakers was enormous.

Because of the extreme time frame – I only had a few minutes for each of the 60 to 70 speakers – I had to develop a method that would work for everyone regardless of their experience level.

This experience inspired me to develop what has become a very successful eight-minute coaching process.

One on one, in a very short time, I covered much of what you are about to read. You will soon how to use that knowledge to jump ahead on the corporate ladder.

In their everyday lives, each of these GE Capital
people felt confident speaking to a group of
10 peers in a meeting room at the home office.
For many of them, English was not their native
language. When the audience changed to include
the company's 600 leaders from around the world,
the pressures obviously changed exponentially.

My job was to provide on-the-job coaching on the
day before the dreaded speech. I "inherited" them
after they had met with the graphics designer in
another room to discuss the look and feel of their
presentation.

The basics of each speech included:

- A lectern
- The speaker's scribbled notes
- "3 ups" - their graphics, printed three per page
  with space for notes
- Graphics projected on a big screen
  behind them

The speakers advanced their own graphics using a wireless remote control connected to two computers located backstage.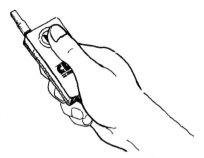

My "classroom" was the empty ballroom and stage. Each of the presenters stood there rattling their notes at the lectern before an "audience" of 600 empty chairs. Clearly, they would rather be outside playing golf with their colleagues.

I knew those empty chairs were part of their nervousness. I knew each of my "students" was imagining their bosses sitting in every one of those chairs. To help ease their minds, I placed myself physically between them and the empty seats in the ballroom. Next, I looked them in the eye, and used the next eight minutes to coach them on giving an effective presentation.

Were my GE Capital presenters still nervous, even after my eight-minute coaching? Absolutely. But after working with me, they knew what to do with all that energy. (And you soon will know what they learned.)

At this point I learned the value of the pressure on each one of them. They would be able to focus on each of the tools I handed them and impress their boss – and themselves.

During the years I have been in business, many other clients have learned how to make better presentations. In many instances, my mid-level to senior executive clients found that the time and effort invested in delivering an effective presentation yielded big returns. As I mentioned earlier, it helped them to advance their careers and to increase their personal value within their companies. Many of my clients worked for leading organizations such as:

- Taco Bell
- DuPont
- Lockheed
- Monsanto
- Corinthian Colleges
- Comcast
- J&J Companies
- Kelley Services

CHAPTER ONE

OK, so now what do I do?

Unless you attended the best MBA schools, you were never trained to make large audience presentations. Even experienced speakers sometimes forget this is an acquired skill.

But how do you acquire this skill? The same way you get to Carnegie Hall: practice, practice, practice.

But first, you need some basic skills and understanding.

You need to understand:

- Who is my audience?
- What are the three ideas I need to deliver?
- What is my "call to action" for the audience?
- How do I ensure success?

Vince Lombardi was named "Coach of the 20th Century" by ESPN. This famed Green Bay Packers coach is remembered for his dedication, his infectious enthusiasm and his unforgettable quotes that continue to echo in locker rooms around the world. Such as …

> *"Practice does not make perfect. Only perfect practice makes perfect."*

Lombardi knew that even successful football players require on-the-job training when they move to a new team. At the opening of every football season practice, he would acknowledge to the rookies and veterans alike a fundamental first step in football basics by showing them the ball and announcing:

"This is a football."

This book will present on-the-job skills as basic as Lombardi's "this is a football." It will also offer equally important guidance in your executive development and career advancement.

Speaking in public is not easy for most people.

As Gerard Blair ays in his *Starting to Manage: The Essential Skills*[1]:

> *Consider a simple skill like driving a car. When you were a child, you often saw grown-ups driving. As you sat beside them, you watched their feet moving, sometimes you even held the wheel (before you knew this was illegal). So, was that enough to teach you how to drive? Could you have simply slipped into the driver's seat and taken over?*
>
> *Would you have driven a racing car around a Grand Prix track on your first afternoon? Of course not; someone had to show you how. That is not to say you watched someone do it: someone actually sat down beside you in the passenger seat and helped you acquire that skill.*

Unfortunately, I can't sit down with you as you prepare for your next presentation. But the tools presented in this book will help you acquire the skills you need to deliver your message confidently and professionally.

1   IEEE Engineers Guide to Business, Vol 8.

Getting started

When you discover you have been "chosen" to
speak to a large group, you quickly understand
your on-the-job speech training begins NOW. You
have little time to perfect the ability to deliver
a smart, professional presentation in front of
an audience. This book can help you become
more comfortable making those presentations.
It can lead to that important promotion. It can
lead to greater recognition from your company
leadership.

A formal speech class or Toastmasters will give
you some reference material and a platform on
which to practice, but those who have benefited
from my eight-minute lesson will always do better
at crunch time.

Chances are you chose this book because of two
important factors:

- You have a message to deliver – that is, you've
  been selected to tell people what you know by
  someone who trusts your knowledge of the
  subject matter.
- You have very limited time (under three
  weeks) to prepare for this presentation.

That time frame is actually your friend. It's your
motivation to simplify, simplify, simplify – just
boil the material down to the basics and get the
job done.

- No time to fly cross-country for a scheduled two-day consult with a speech coach.
- No time to videotape your presentation in a class and play it back over and over for critique by your peers.

No time to take chances with your future.

Using my "success" toolbox, you can learn presentation skills on-the-job, and become the speaker who has greater impact on your audience.

Organization: the first tool in the box

The producers of popular TV home makeover shows know the value of organization: there's a place for everything, and everything belongs in its place. You can have the best hand-crafted furniture in the world, but if your magazines and books and the kids' toys and the laundry are all over the place, it still looks like a dump.

The same theory applies to giving a presentation: you can have good material, but it takes organization to make it great!

Create a one-sentence objective

Refer to this sentence throughout the organization process to ensure you meet this goal. Remember, this book is not a complete step-by-step resource for writing a presentation. We can, however, provide some vital how-to's to ensure that your remarks are organized and ready to be effectively delivered.

Next, outline your message. An outline helps you organize your thoughts, and ensures that your message gets across. Another benefit of an outline is that you have an at-a-glance, one-page look at your entire presentation.

No more than 3 "thoughts to remember"

While preparing your outline, select the three points you want the audience to know at the end of your presentation.

By building your presentation around just three points, you ensure that your message is clear, concise, and easy for your audience to remember. Focus on those three points and you'll go a long way toward a successful presentation.

Have you heard about the six-year-old who asked his mother, "Where did I come from?"

The mother goes into the entire birthing process for 10 minutes, only to be interrupted by the six-year-old, "No, Mom, I meant are we from Cleveland?"

Resist the urge to take on "The Meaning of Life" in 20 minutes. Too much information will cloud your real message.

Determine at the outset if you are to present a detailed how-to or an overview from 30,000 feet. Keep that thought as you develop your presentation. This will make a big difference in how you prepare and present.

Write a test script

Next, write out the message. Do this to fill in the outline while you decide how long you need to dwell on any one point. As you write your test script, you will also choose where to place anecdotes or other examples.

Read the full script out loud and record yourself. Time your presentation. As you listen to the playback, you will hear where you need more or less content and how to transition between thoughts. **CUT** material now.

Your test script is a good way to get approval from others on the material you plan to present.

At this stage, don't waste time creating speaker support slides. After all, this is material that will probably end up being cut.

Don't begin production on slides, videos, etc, until the test script is complete

Why not create slides first? Those who insist on making PowerPoint slides as their outline fall into a common trap. They are putting the icing on before the cake is baked. Your message is a coherent story, not a collection of wordy bullet points.

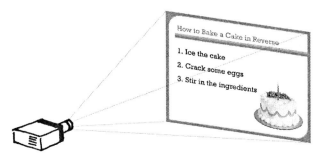

Use less time than you're allotted

Do everything you can to organize your thoughts so your message will take less time than you're allowed. If you are given 20 minutes, use 15. You'll have time to answer questions, or you'll be seen as a hero for finishing without wasting time.

If you're given a 40-minute time allotment, your first question should be, "Why 40 minutes?"

Consider this: a multi-million dollar Super Bowl commercial tells the important story of a new product in 30 seconds. *Do you really need 40 minutes to tell your story?*

If you must fill more than 20 minutes, don't try to do it all yourself. Get some help:

- Include relevant video clips in your script
- Enlist other people to share in your presentation
- Develop a good, relevant audience activity
- Use the time wisely to "reinforce" the message that should only take 20 minutes to tell.
- Consider a question-and-answer session following your presentation.

**Tell the audience what your message will be.
Tell 'em your message.
Tell 'em what you've told 'em.**

You've probably heard this saying before. Though simplistic, it's great advice. Adhering to this little bromide,[2] which is really a streamlined version of Aristotle's ideas on giving speeches, will keep you on track as you prepare your presentation. It will make your audience comfortable and secure because they'll know where you're headed. And it will help you stay focused as you make your presentation.

Include a call to action for your audience

If your audience is successfully motivated or informed by your presentation, they will want something to do as a result. Good calls to action include completing a task, creating a team, measuring performance – anything that's a good challenge *and* relates to your message.

Ask for audience questions if time permits

If you crafted your message properly, taking into consideration the audience's knowledge as you wrote your test script, there may be no questions.

Handling Q&A requires some special training as well. Read more about Q&A in Chapter Four.

---

2   Source: Proven Techniques for Creating Presentations That Get Results 1998 by Daria Price Bowman.

Say "thank you"

Always end your presentation with a sincere "thank you" before you introduce the next presenter or turn it back to the host or moderator.

This is an appropriate opportunity for the audience to applaud.

Introduce the next person

Find out the next presenter's message. Use that information to create a short, sincere welcome for him or her.

CHAPTER TWO

From Outline to Presentation

Once you've created an outline and test script, it's time to fine-tune your presentation.

Most of my clients work from their slides without notes.

Those with less preparation time use either written notes alongside 3-ups of their graphics, or a full-blown, sentence-by-sentence script. Use the method that feels most comfortable for you.

Script format

Your script should be organized using the following guidelines.

- ## Use 16 point type – see how readable it is?

- Always use upper and lower case type. The "ALL CAPS" type was developed in the 1940s for the old-style Associated Press and United Press International machines that fed news wires to radio and television news departments. To be more efficient, the type was all capital letters. ALL-CAP NOTES ARE DIFFICULT TO READ.

To be successful, you should be able to glance down at a sentence, and look up to deliver it. Use a 3-inch wide column for your message, set 3 inches in from the left side of the page. If the copy is wider than your eyes can capture on one quick glance, it's useless.

- Only use the top two thirds of the page. Anything printed on the bottom of the page forces you to look down. Your audience sees only the top of your head.

- Number the pages. Murphy's Law[3] dictates that the speaker who arrives on stage without numbered pages is guaranteed to drop the notes and be unable to reassemble them without a serious period of embarrassment.

- Do not staple the pages. You'll want to "slide" the pages from one to the next. If you turn your pages, sooner or later you'll find your audience "counting pages" instead of hearing your presentation. Invariably, you will bump the microphone with your page turning. That is very embarrassing.

- Do not use a notebook or binder to hold your pages. Turning pages in a binder is noisy and distracting.

---

3   Murphy's Law: If anything can go wrong, it will.

Script template

If you must use a script, prepare it properly. Send me an e-mail[4] requesting the Word template for a useful script format that follows the recommendations provided on the previous section.

```
                                        Client
                                        Project
  _____

  Microsoft Word
  Version 7.0a

                    This format is designed for use in

                    Microsoft Word Version 5.1,6.x. or

                    7.0x. Styles in Word define the font,

                    size, line spacing and other

                    formatting attributes.

  Document Structure

                    Process notes or production steps

                    in this document are shown in copy

                    / bullet style.

                    Other content and explanation is in

                    copy style.

                    This font is 18pt Helvetica.




  _____
  Writer's name        Draft # __ 5/7/2008  2:05 PM        1
```

Organizing your presentation

Whether you are using slides, notes, or a word-for-word script, you need to become familiar with your overall presentation. A word-for-word script should not become a crutch that you end up actually reading word-for-word. Even if you're promising them a sure-fire way to lose 20 pounds in 20 days,

No one
wants
to
see
and
hear
you
read
your
message
sentence
by
sentence
for
20
minutes.

Your brain is always busy, which doesn't always help your presentation

All the speed-reading programs refer to huge numbers, quoting the brain's processing speed. Their goal is to demonstrate how much faster you can read and comprehend with their training.

While I know I can learn to process more words per minute when reading, I can't speak any faster than 150 words per minute.[5] How do you handle YOUR additional processing speed and the AUDIENCE's ability to think a lot faster than you could talk? Once you understand this imbalance, you need to control those thoughts that interrupt delivering your message.

You don't have the luxury to think about last week's BBQ, next week's performance review, or how nervous you are.

Your presentation needs to be scintillating enough to keep your audience's distracting thoughts at bay as well.

---

5 In The Art of Speaking Science, Lisa Marshall says: "When making presentations I speak at approximately 145-160 words per minute (wpm), while an average American English speaker engaged in a friendly conversation speaks at a rate of approximately 110–150 wpm. (Interestingly, publishers recommend books on tape to be voiced at 150-160 wpm, auctioneers are generally 250-400 wpm, while the average reading rate is about 200-300 wpm)."

Nerves: the tool you may not recognize

Nerves may be your most valuable tool. Being nervous means you have lots of energy. A key to success is the realization that excess energy can be channeled into giving a better presentation.

Let's consider the facts about your presentation:

- You live, breathe, and work this message every day.
- The words and phrases are those you use in your everyday vocabulary.
- You've given this message to small groups of people dozens of times.

Bottom line: for most presentations, you've actually given the *exact same message* to friends and family when they ask the question "What are you working on now?"

Even so, being nervous is completely understandable. This is completely different. You're speaking on a stage in front of your peers and your boss or important customers. If you weren't nervous, I'd be a little worried for you.

Nervousness indicates you're anxious to do a good job. Even seasoned performers get nervous. But they've learned to *come to grips with their nervousness.*

Nervousness, if ignored or not handled properly, will make you appear unprepared and fidgety. As a result, you distract your audience from your message.

Key signs of nervousness include pacing the stage, not knowing what to do with your hands, saying the word "um" to fill in the blanks, and losing your train of thought.

How can you capture all those nervous twitches and impulses and channel that energy into something useful? Use that energy as a *tool* to your advantage.

- Find a real, or imagined, person in the fifth row and "talk" to them. Really talk to them. The entire room will feel as if you're speaking to them as well.
- Move your attention to another person only after you have finished a complete thought and feel your point is received well.
- Remember: this is not a stadium pep rally.
- Remember: this is not the Gettysburg Address.[6]
- Control your thoughts by eliminating mental distractions.

---

6   Delivered by President Lincoln at Gettysburg on November 19, 1863.

Part of your fear is wondering "What will the audience think of me?"

Relax. Your audience is not afraid of you, or jealous of you. They know that, at any minute, they could be in your shoes.

Your audience recognizes four key aspects about you being on stage:

- You're the expert chosen by someone to talk about this subject.

- They're glad they're not up there.

- They're willing to let you do whatever you need to do to be successful.

- They want you to be successful.

The only reason your audience will become critical of you is if they see your thoughts aren't organized, your graphics aren't coordinated, or you look uncomfortable.

The best way to use your nervous energy and address your audience in a positive, professional way is to *practice your presentation.*

The practice tool

It might seem obvious, but many people do not recognize the critical need to practice their presentations. Public speaking is like any other skill: you only get better with practice.

Take time to rehearse your material out loud, not reading it silently. Silent reading only lulls you into thinking you know the material.

The best way to determine how well you know your material is to lock yourself in the bathroom, face the mirror, and speak your presentation out loud.

- Speaking the material <u>out loud</u> also forces you to work on transitions. Is there a logical progression from one thought to another?

- How often can you look in the mirror as you practice? The more you see your own eyes, the better you know your stuff.

- Your goal is to know the material well enough that you only need to <u>glance</u> at the next note to be reminded of the next group of thoughts.

Good practice out loud in front of a mirror will reveal if you are able to deliver all the material while looking yourself in the eye and while actually communicating your message. Do that a few times, and you'll come to the stage with full confidence you know your material.

Your audience, on the other hand, will immediately recognize an unrehearsed presentation. They will perceive you as disorganized, and disrespectful of their time and the importance of the event. If you present without having spoken the message out loud, you, too, will be embarrassed when you find your words don't flow and you stumble for thoughts.

That eight minutes

You recall me highlighting my eight-minute instruction? Well, that was my portion of the preparation. My part was easy.

Now it's time for you to take a few hours on your own.

Here are more tools for your toolbox. Using them properly will allow you to focus on your message.

Home base for your hands

In my eight-minute lesson, I ask my students to stand away from the lectern and keep their hands at their sides. After a very short 10 seconds, with the thought of an audience in front of them, they report that each hand feels like a ton of bricks.

Try it yourself.

Stand up in front of a few people and keep your hands to your sides. After a few seconds, think about moving your hands.

The thought of what to do with your hands is distracting from your message. In fact, you have so many choices of where to put your hands, it can get you off-message quickly.

I developed a "home base for your hands."

Home base is two hands with bended elbows just above your belt. As soon as you try that, another feeling comes to mind. "This feels really silly."

Progress!

Of course it feels silly. It is only home base. Take a second to feel silly – then, USE THE HANDS in front of you – naturally, easily. It is so much simpler to use them from home base than anywhere else.

What a relief.

I have seen speech training classes where novice presenters were told where in the script to gesture. That is nuts. If you are truly "involved" in the message, your hands jump out of home base to support natural gestures.

Do it yourself. Stand up, put your hands by your side, and start talking. The minute you start thinking about something else – like what to do with your hands – you get distracted.

I want you to instantly recognize when your hands enter your thought process. Don't waste a nano-second thinking about them. Go to home base.

Some things become instinctive, once you have the knowledge. You know not to put wet food in a hot frying pan because you'll get splattered.

Likewise, the minute you put your hands where they aren't supposed to, or you begin wandering around the stage, you need to RECOGNIZE it – and make the necessary corrections to get back on-message without being distracted.

Get comfortable with your hands at home base.
I've coached speakers who put their hands in their
pockets and instantly pulled them out to get them
back to home base and to the message.

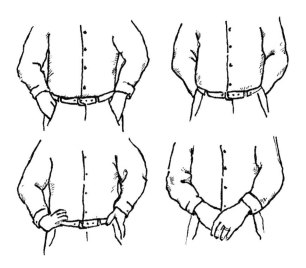

I love seeing the quick smile of recognition when
their hands return to home base and they continue
unflustered.

Train yourself to recognize the things you're
unconsciously doing that will hijack your
message.

It takes practice to manage your distractions

Think about when you're driving a car. As you drive, you are actually processing a myriad of things but your most important task is safe driving. It is often compromised by turning on the windshield wipers, talking on the cell phone, taking a sip of coffee, thinking about your kid's baseball game, hitting the brakes at a traffic light. You must manage these distractions as you drive. That's what you are doing in a speech: managing your distractions.

In most states there are laws restricting drivers from the distraction of using a cell phone or texting. You will need to be careful not to "crash" during your brief presentation – without legislation.

One law of presenting should be: stumbling over a sentence is proof you're not paying attention.

It's a GOOD thing. If you're just going through the motions and you can't put a sentence together, **you really are going through the motions**. Stop.

Tell yourself, "It's OK to stop. It's a good thing I stumbled this early in my presentation. I have time to recover." Then, take a deep breath and go back to work.

CHAPTER THREE
Practice, Practice, Practice

Your success is in direct correlation to the time spent practicing

In his book *Risk, Originality & Virtuosity: The Keys to a Perfect 10,*[7] Olympic Gold Medal gymnast Peter Vidmar talks about the importance of practice if you want to win a gold medal.

> *Your task is not nearly as difficult as winning an Olympic medal but you do have to worry a little about your overall score. After all, the people in the audience might be your current boss – or your future boss.*

Fortunately, you're delivering material you know, and you have an empathetic audience; They sure don't want to change places with you!

...umm

As an audience member, have you ever started counting the "...umms" in someone's speech? These are called discourse markers. In some speeches, it's too easy to count the distractions, (a speaker's pacing, playing with their hair, losing their place, or not making eye contact) and, in the process, you miss the message.

---

7   Risk, Originality & Virtuosity: The Keys to a Perfect 10, Publisher - Leading Authorities Inc. 2002

Only by recording your rehearsal and listening to it as an audience member will you eliminate the "...umms" and other distractions. Be sure to make notes along the way.

To memorize or not

In my experience, attempting to memorize a presentation only adds more pressure – and interrupts your ability to deliver your message.

Remember:

- This is your material
- Your words
- Your everyday message ... this time, delivered to 600 people

Don't memorize your presentation. The process of recalling the material in order will distract you from the message itself.

On the other hand, know your first and last sentence

I have seen more than one presenter with his head glued to the notes reading his opening line, "Good morning, my name is <Insert Name Here> and I am glad to be here this morning"!

As you approach the end, take a deep breath, look directly at the audience and deliver your final sentence. Everyone has some ability to memorize. But why take the energy to do so? Organize your thoughts, make your notes easy to read, and craft your PowerPoint slides so that they assist you along the way.

I've been told memorizing is a crutch to help you get through the presentation. This is not true. You don't memorize a discussion with your friends and colleagues about your job and objectives.

On stage during your presentation

Don't make your presentation "bigger" than it needs to be.

Watch any network anchor deliver the evening news. You can sit anywhere in your living room and feel he is delivering the news *directly to you and you alone.* The anchor looks you right in the eye, he's not shouting, he's calm, cool, and collected.

That speaking style will serve you well. Look into the audience and deliver a thought to every "one" person.

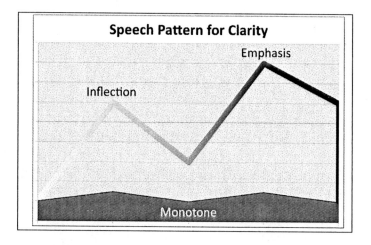

Use inflection changes to help you highlight the key points. When talking about something you think is exciting, show you are excited!

Also use pauses. Yes, the dreaded pause.

Try talking to an audience of friends or peers. While doing so, take a breath and contemplate what you are about to say. That may take two seconds. It will seem natural with your friends, but a lifetime on stage.

Audiences want to know you are thinking while you're up there. Take a pause. You will collect your audience as well as your thoughts.

The eye contact tool

Speakers get "no points" by forcing sweeping eye contact of the entire audience. You've seen this happen: The speaker looks down at his notes, reads a line, looks up, smiles, looks down again, reads another line.

What's your opinion of this speaker? He sure doesn't know his presentation. He most certainly hasn't practiced. The overall effect is someone who isn't prepared to make an effective presentation.

The audience wants you to look up and deliver the material. Look down for a brief moment, only long enough to get the next thought. Then look up and deliver the message looking at your audience.

Many national political candidates read all of their major speeches. That in itself is not unusual. But when a candidate favors the two teleprompter glass reflections so much, they very seldom look at the audience in the middle. To me that is very distracting. I'm over here ... look at me!

Walking and talking: tool or distraction?

Stand still or walk around? Some seasoned veterans tell me they have to walk around when they talk. When I explain what the audience sees, they give it a second thought … or two.

While on stage, you can walk, but you better have a reason to do so.

Purposeless wandering distracts your audience from your message and dissipates important energy you need to use to communicate your message.

Ever see a caged tiger at the zoo? That's what's you look like when you pace up and down the stage. It's just another interruption to your message.

Instead, use all that wasted energy for your message. Adopt this stance:

- Stand still with your feet planted about shoulder-width apart.
- Keep your knees bent slightly.
- Present a relaxed image.
- Use your upper body to gesture at your audience.
- Use your hands for effective delivery.

When does on-stage walking work? When there's a reason for it.

- Purposeful walking to one side of the stage or another works if you stay there.
- Deliver a full thought or two on that side of the stage.
- Finish your thought before going to another spot on stage.

I have worked with many of the major speakers on the corporate event circuit, including ESPN commentator and football coach Lou Holtz. During Lou's sound check, he asked, "Where do you want me?"

He stood where I indicated, spoke his 61 minutes, and brought the audience to their feet, as usual. Not once during that hour did he move one iota from the "mark" I had taped on the stage.

Really PROJECTING your image

On some occasions, you will have the advantage (or disadvantage) of having live video images of you projected on a big screen behind you as you speak.

Image Magnification (IMAG) is a tool that allows audiences to see you and look into your eyes as you present. Know where the camera is, so you can use IMAG to full advantage.

In my experience, 80% of a large audience will take advantage of watching the video image of you as you speak. That image may be projected adjacent to any graphics.

When using IMAG, talk to your audience the way you rehearsed, but occasionally – when you want to make a point to everyone in the room – look straight into the lens of the IMAG camera and deliver your point.

With IMAG, you will especially want to stand in one place to deliver your message. That BIG picture of you will keep the image of you from waist up no matter what you do. So, if you're wandering around the stage, the image remains the same and you force the camera to follow you. The result is a moving background on the big screen, which is very distracting for the audience.

Audiences report seasickness as the background seems to move back and forth endlessly on IMAG. Help minimize that distraction by standing in one place and delivering your message.

Don't look at the screen!

It is rude to turn and look, read, or point at the screen. You may see where you are pointing, but the audience is left guessing. You also tend to turn your back on the audience and walk into the projection beam, which adds a shadow on the screen. If there are two screens in the room, it's important to indicate on the graphics where the data or image is.

- While making eye contact with your audience, refer to the upper left, right or middle of the screen. They will follow you.
- If you have a preview screen in front of you, the directions (left, right, etc.) are the same to you and the audience.

Pause now and then for your audience to catch up with your thinking as they look over the graphic.

What to wear?

If your image is being projected on IMAG, avoid the following on-camera distractions:

- Tight checked patterns or thin lines (these patterns create distracting moiré images on camera)
- White or black jackets or sweaters (TV cameras hate large areas of black or white)
- Turtleneck (you will need to have a place to place the lavaliere microphone if you anticipate using one. A button-front shirt will serve you better).
- A shiny face or forehead. Everyone looks different under theatrical lights. If it's offered, take advantage of powder makeup to minimize any shine on your face, forehead, or thinning hair line.
- With the adoption of HD video, you will want to be concerned about how you look on the big screen and subsequent viewings.

Discuss a "dress style" for the presentations with your fellow presenters, whether it's a business suit, sport jacket or business casual. In some tropical venues (Hawaii or Florida), more casual wear may be appropriate.

Avoid the risk involved in wearing a costume. You may think a costume will sell your point, but some of your audience may not get it. You will also have to live with the after-life of any photos or videos in your costume. Do you really want to star in a YouTube video?

If you want to use a costume to help your message, keep it simple. You must rehearse in the costume to test the lighting and microphone techniques if you are on a big stage.

Using props

Props, awards, and demonstrations can often help make your presentation more interesting.

All props must be large enough to be seen by the entire audience or by the IMAG cameras. It must be seen above the heads of the first row in the audience. Riding in on a bicycle will be funny to only a few people down front who see you as you ride by. Others seated further back in the room will not get the joke.

Anything that happens below your waist on stage is a wasted gesture to your audience. They just won't see it.

In the late 1990s, we presented the famous Taco Bell Chihuahua to an audience of 650 people. The grand entrance had to be staged six feet off the floor since the audience was expected to be standing as the celebrity dog made its triumphant entrance from the audience to the stage. Had the dog walked in on the ballroom floor, 99% of the audience would not have enjoyed the spectacle.

Carefully plan where the props will be when you need them. I prefer to have someone ready at the edge of the stage to hand the prop or award up to the stage.

If you hold up anything to the audience, be sure to hold it high and close to you.

One CEO had so many props he ducked down to pick them up, one at a time. Then, when he finished using each prop, he placed them one-by-one on the lectern top. At one point, you couldn't see him!

Know what you are going to do with the props when you're finished using them. Put them on a side table, hand them to someone, or put them in your pocket. Don't let them pile up and block you from the audience.

Focus on your message

You know the material; now, you are ready to share it with others.

Many people get bored with their own voice. It often happens after significant practice and rehearsal. Don't let yourself become bored!

Think about the cast of the Broadway hit *A Chorus Line.* The people who paid good money to see the Broadway May 21, 1975, opening of *A Chorus Line* saw the same show as the people who paid good money to see the closing night show on April 28ʼ 1991,[8] The End of the Line 6,137 and final performance. The cast delivered the same excitement opening night as they did *sixteen years later,* because, for the audience, ***every night is opening night.***

Like every audience of *A Chorus Line,* your audience has never heard your "show." They're hearing it for the first time. Deliver your message with the same enthusiasm every time.

On multi-city road shows, I always prompt the presenters not to be bored with their material. Every audience deserves an "Opening Night" performance.

---

8   http://www.achorusline.org/timeline.html.

Concluding your presentation

You've said what you came to say. Now it's time to give the audience an opportunity to applaud your performance. Then thank your audience.

Really mean it. Show a smile or genuine relief if you feel it, but this is their cue you are finished and they can demonstrate their appreciation. Wait for a beat or two, then introduce the next speaker.

Stay at your place on stage during the transition.

Allow the audience to see you exchange pleasantries (and the graphics clicker if necessary).

Walk behind the new presenter and exit the stage.

"Did I just swallow a fly?" and other distractions

There are so many distractions to deal with when you are on stage – everything from an audience member hacking away until you think you should call 911, to that pesky fly that keeps buzzing around you, to the fact that the laundry used too much starch on your shirt.

While rehearsing for a convention presentation, it is not unusual to do so while the hotel staff is moving tables and chairs, setting up for the next event while you are on stage practicing your presentation. This is a good test of your ability to concentrate on your material.

Mind drift: cause and effect

At the risk of repeating myself earlier in Chapter 2, your brain is ALWAYS busy. This is perhaps the most important challenge giving a presentation. Before you can appreciate the need to eliminate distractions, you should understand your ability to focus on just the message.

- People usually fast talk at about 150 words per minute.
- People usually normally think at 600 to 800 words per minute.
- So, even if you are paying close attention, you still have tons of free time in your head.

Here is what Brian Thwaits says in his book *THE BIG LEARN: Smart Ways To Use Your Brain*[9]:

> *Because our brains are capable of processing information at incredible speeds (between 1000 and 25000 words per minute), it's no wonder that we so often forget what we read (at an average rate of 250 wpm) and hear (at an average rate of 150 wpm)! We read and listen so slowly that only a very small part of our brain activity is focused on the task at hand.*

It's a problem for you, as a speaker – because you too, can go into mind drift during your presentation. Your multitasking ability will interrupt your message. Stay on point and focus on your message.

If you're pacing the floor, punctuating your message with "um," or misusing your hands, you're giving your audience something else to think about. They, too, can process more than 600 words a minute – yet you're only speaking at 125 words a minute. So, they have all that excess to think about, too. It's up to you to keep them on YOUR message.

---

9   THE BIG LEARN: Smart Ways To Use Your Brain, Trafford Publishing, 2007

Your brain is simply teeming with electrical energy right now. Those electrical signals are moving at fantastic speeds, yet the act of speaking delivers information much slower.

What do you do with the excess capacity? You can't talk faster, although I've seen many try – and fail miserably - at getting their message across.

Remember, your goal isn't to FINISH. Your goal is to impart knowledge and/or motivate an audience.

Conquer your mind drift by crafting a presentation that involves active listening: ask questions, share interests, solve problems, and ask for a show of support where appropriate. All of these tools will help keep you focused on your audience, and your audience focused on you.

Use all your energy to deliver the message.

The A Team in charge

A few years ago, a corporate client called with an interesting challenge to my 8-minute training technique. I had coached all of their executives for more than a dozen years.

This company holds quarterly meetings in their headquarters building, with 350 employees in attendance. Typically these meetings are addressed by company executives.

The challenge they gave me? Turn the presentations at one meeting over to the Administrative Team (A Team): the people who support the executives.

These "admins" schedule their bosses, maintain their very busy calendars, and coordinate the business lives of very successful executives. They often know everything that's going on within their department. I've always counted on them to grant me access when I needed it.

In my first meeting with them as a group, these busy people were frightened about the task before them. None of them had ever spoken to a group larger than 10, and then only for a few minutes.

Each admin was given the charge to host a 10-minute portion of the meeting with an opening message supported by PowerPoint, and then introduce the next speaker or moderate a panel of other supporting staff members.

I explained all the tools covered in this book. We then went through the "what do I do with these?" exercise with hands and other basics.

I told them how to develop their message and how to practice. Two days later, I met again with six excited people. They had crafted their message and their graphics, and they had followed my instructions on the need to practice.

Now, for the first time, they rehearsed with their graphics and microphone in the empty auditorium. They practiced their transitions to each other as I reinforced the training.

You know the result, of course. These admins – who came to me with virtually no experience or confidence as public speakers – were amazed at how successful they had been. An appreciative audience gave them a standing ovation, and the accolades kept coming for weeks afterward.

One enthusiastic woman explained she had rehearsed in front of a bathroom mirror (just as I have advised you to do). Then she assembled her husband, 2-year-old and 13-year-old in the living room and rehearsed her presentation to that audience the night before.

In fact, her 13-year-old daughter had a chance to be in the audience during this woman's presentation at work; she was so proud to see her mom do so well and receive a standing ovation. The two of them had such big grins, I will never forget that moment.

Needless to say, these women of power within the organization are now regarded with additional respect by everyone who attended that meeting.

Their confidence on stage reinforced how knowledgeable they are about the company and its objectives in a very public way.

CHAPTER FOUR
Using Technology & Other Tools

Resist the temptation to write your speech in PowerPoint

Using the PowerPoint software on to organize your speech is the immediate path to bad graphics. Though it seems an easy tool to organize your thoughts, the outline created in PowerPoint often leads to useless graphics. Ideal graphics are intended to support your presentation not be your presentation.

Instead, use pencil and paper or a Word document to begin your outline, and then your content.

Graphics: friend or foe

I have worked with former PepsiCo executives who were selected to manage the organization's restaurant division. The company eventually spun off its restaurants—forming a brand new company known as TRICON Inc. (now YUM! Brands), and their holdings included KFC, Pizza Hut, and Taco Bell.

In small groups, the PepsiCo methodology required every presenter to create a "deck" of overhead transparencies or "foils" to use on an overhead projector.

This "deck" was intended to include everything the speaker needed to know about a subject on one page. Decks were also used as a leave-behind to explain everything to a follow-up audience of one person, who would then read the deck.

The title at the top of each page was often a sentence describing the information to follow. This material was read like a page in a book.

If you must leave behind a "deck" for this purpose, create two sets of graphics: one to support your presentation, the other to leave behind.

Graphics used for your presentation are not the same as a deck

These days, all "decks" are created using PowerPoint from Microsoft. The overhead projector has been replaced with a video projector and laptop.

The PowerPoint tool: use it wisely

Use PowerPoint slides to amplify your message, not to *be* your message.

My favorite insult is when a presenter tells his audience, "I know you aren't going to be able to read this tiny print, but I'm going to put it up anyway."

Why? So you can read it to the audience? Don't insult them. If you plan to simply read your slides and call it your presentation, why not just mail it in?

- Use your speaking skills to bring your message to life.
- Use the graphics to reinforce your message. Use photos and illustrations instead of words where possible.
- Countless studies demonstrate an audience learns much more when they *hear* a message and *see* supporting information *together*.

PowerPoint turned 20 in 2007

In a column for *The Wall Street Journal*, Lee Gomes celebrated the anniversary of PowerPoint and what the designers (Robert Gaskins and Dennis Austin) of the program were thinking 20 years later[10].

> *Perhaps the most scathing criticism comes from the Yale graphics guru Edward Tufte, who says the software "elevates format over content, betraying an attitude of commercialism that turns everything into a sales pitch."*
>
> *He even suggested PowerPoint played a role in the Columbia shuttle disaster, as some vital technical news was buried in an otherwise upbeat slide.*

---

10   WSJ June 20, 2007 – Portals by Lee Gomes.

One of the problems, Gaskin and Austin say, is that with PowerPoint now bundled with Office, vastly more people have access to the program than the relatively small group of salespeople for which is was intended. When video projectors became small and cheap, just about every room on earth became PowerPoint-ready.

If they have a lament, it's that complaints about PowerPoint are usually not about the software but about bad presentations. It's just like the printing press, says Mr. Austin. It enabled all sorts of garbage to be printed.

Gaskins continues to say:

A PowerPoint presentation was never supposed to be the entire proposal, just a quick summary of something longer and better thought out. He cites as an example his original business plan for the program: 53 densely argued pages long. The dozen or so slides that accompanied it were but the highlights.

Since then, he complains, "a lot of people in business have given up writing the documents. They just write the presentations, which are summaries without the detail, without the backup. A lot of people don't like the intellectual rigor of actually doing the work."

Now grade-school children turn in book reports via PowerPoint. The men call that an abomination. Children, they emphatically agree, need to think and write in complete paragraphs.

From overhead projector to PowerPoint on laptops

When the overhead projector ruled the boardroom and group events, the presenter enjoyed having total control of the content. All he or she had to do was simply copy  the pages of a book or computer printout and slap the transparency on the screen. To pace yourself, you could always see where you were going by sneaking a peak at the next transparency.

With PowerPoint, that advantage has disappeared. You have a few choices to "prompt" yourself on what comes next:

- Take a chance on what the next slide is.
- Rely on good rehearsals to know your material.
- Refer to your printed copies of your slides.
- Set up another laptop one frame ahead.

Try that last suggestion: Use your laptop, fed to a projector, and talk to your first slide. Wouldn't it be nice to know precisely what comes next?

Using a second laptop

When the budget allows, we provide our clients with two laptop computers loaded with the identical slide show. The second laptop is always set a frame ahead in each presentation. As the presenter advances a slide on one laptop, the second laptop (not seen by the audience) also advances, and now the presenter knows what's coming up.

This works best, of course, when you are prepared enough to present without notes or a lectern.

Even more powerful presentations are accomplished with the laptops off stage. Both computers advance every time you trigger a cue.

With this system, each computer feeds its video monitor positioned on the floor in front of the stage. The one monitor (the program monitor, which is the same image as that seen on the audience screen) shows the slide you're on.

The other monitor (the preview monitor) shows the slide you're going to next. It helps to place a big "X" in masking tape across the stage-left monitor, to differentiate the two monitors. This will provide just enough image for you to know what's coming up, without getting confused.

Use a wireless remote control device to advance the prime. Have someone else advance the second computer with your preview frame.[11] Now you "magically" talk to the audience with full eye contact and only an occasional glimpse to the monitors on the floor to check what's coming up next.

---

11 PerfectCue device by D'San Corp. PerfectCue is a light and sound signaling system. It enables a speaker to send cues to an operator using a wireless hand-held actuator.

Place the monitors 2 to 3 feet off the floor. If the monitors are high enough, 98 percent of your audience will think you are talking to people in the front row instead of glancing at the monitors. Don't be concerned they are too high. The front row will look over them and forget the monitors are there. Those in the rows behind will never see them.

Only when you are well-rehearsed, you can pull this off without totally damaging your credibility. Otherwise, your audience will know you are reading rather than presenting.

Who should advance your slides?

One client has a colleague advance his slides. Although they create the presentation together and rehearse it often, the presenter inevitably has to use up some of his focus wondering when and if his partner will change the slide.

If you are not using a script, advancing your own slides is the only safe way to insure you are on-message.

Why do I have to work so hard?

In some cases, I am challenged by new clients who are speaking without a script and don't want to advance his/her own graphics. They simply don't want to work that hard, trying to remember everything in their presentation *and* advancing the slides.

Based on years of working with alternative solutions, I recommend you advance your own slides.

In fact, I give presenters a wireless device with ONLY ONE BUTTON: FORWARD. It is common for someone to ask, "Where is the reverse button? What do I do if I get out of order and need to go back?"

I explain to them, "Like life itself, there is only a FORWARD button. If you lose your place, just announce to the audience you messed up and ask me nicely (I am in the back of the room) to back up a slide".

If you have two buttons or more on your wireless device, tape over all but the FORWARD button. It is safer for you.

After that information sinks in, it becomes clear that owning your graphics is necessary for a successful presentation.

Stay focused on your message for the entire 20 minutes you are presenting. That includes making sure your slides coordinate with what you are saying.

If a colleague advances your slides, you lose any attempt at spontaneity. One drift away from the rehearsed message will add an element of uncertainty. "Will he need me to say a key word to advance the slide? What WAS that key word anyway?"

One of my favorite clients learned this the hard way. For years, he insisted his colleagues advance the slides during his presentation. Once he took control, everyone commented how much better his presentations had become.

Lecterns: valuable tool, or not?

In the ideal world, you know your presentation backward and forward. You've practiced in front of a mirror; you even know when to pause to let the message sink in. Your jokes are well timed, and you're presenting the requisite three thoughts – no more, no less.

Using a lectern properly is the next tool – or not.

A lectern is intended to support a book or notes. Place your notes – not your full weight! – on the lectern!

When I coach presenters on stage, I love watching their faces when I tell them, "The lectern[12] should hold PAPERS, NOT PEOPLE."

The minute you hold onto the lectern, you've just shut down your image to the world. You've also closed down your *breathing*.

Any "comfort" you may feel hanging onto the lectern breaks your connection with the audience.

---

12 Strictly speaking, a podium is a raised platform on which you stand to give a speech; the piece of furniture on which you place your notes and behind which you stand is a lectern. – Common Errors in English Usage" by Paul Brians, William, James Co. March 2003.

You can't project a good image hunched over a lectern

I have been known to give the following exaggerated example to seasoned and new speakers:

> *There's 220 volts of electricity running through the lectern. It's OK to use one hand to follow your progress, but the minute you "close the circuit" by also placing the free hand on the lectern, you will be electrocuted.*

Clearly, the lectern serves a purpose and it takes practice to use it well.

Make the lectern work for you

- Place your notes as high on the lectern as possible. During your presentation, audience eye contact is critical, so do everything within your power to keep from looking down further than necessary. And make sure your pages are in numerical order!

- Never place your notes in a binder. Turning pages is noisy and you risk either the pages or the binder itself hitting the microphone and waking everyone up.
- Stand tall on the stage and keep one hand on your place in the notes. Use the other hand to gesture naturally. If you don't need to keep your place in your notes, take a half-step back from the lectern, and speak as if the lectern is not there.
- Don't expect someone else to deliver your notes to the lectern. Take your notes with you from your seat. And don't leave them on the lectern for the next person to deal with.
- When you are well prepared and rehearsed, you will notice the lectern disappear. You can ignore this obstacle if you are ready. Walk away from the lectern when you can. It is only there for your notes, not a place to hide behind.

A good investment

The best "holder" for your notes is made by Brewer-Cantelmo Co.[13] Their Script-Master box effectively holds your stack of notes on one side while providing a "well" to slide the pages, smoothly and silently, without the audience ever noting you have moved on.

---

13 Brewer-Cantelmo Co, Inc; (212) 685-1200; http://www.brewer-cantelmo.com/xpage2a.shtml.

Last words on Lecterns

Most successful speakers know their material well enough that they don't need notes or a lectern.

It is always fun for me to greet a newcomer at one of my client events. The first question is often "Where is the podium?" I encourage them to consider the power they will have over the audience if they are not standing behind this obstacle.

If you are presenting to an audience that is accustomed to seeing presenters stuck behind a lectern, you will amaze them when you step away without a net because you are well prepared and know the value of direct audience contact.

At one of my long-term client's meetings, all presenters use wireless microphones, and they have all replaced the lectern with an inconspicuous music stand, or a tiny table to hold the occasional note or prop or glass of water. This leaves them free to address the audience directly, without a lectern coming between them. With proper rehearsal, this should be all you need.

Microphone mechanics

While we're on the subject of lectern etiquette, we need to include a few words about proper use of the microphone (mic).[14]

Most of my coaching will help you eliminate ANYTHING that distracts from your message. If you don't have a working mic, or your notes are lost, you will have to go on. The more prepared you are for your presentation, the easier it is to deal with annoyances.

---

14 The industry shortcut for "microphone" is mic.

Important checklist before your presentation

- Test the mic before the audience arrives.
- Know you may be surprised by the speaker system when you hear your voice bounce back from the walls for the first time.
- Ask the organizer if you can use a wireless mic so you are not locked to the lectern.
- If you are going to use a wireless mic, be certain you know where the "wired" backup mic is located, in case radio interference renders the wireless mic unusable, which can and does happen.
- Don't "blow" into a microphone to test it. If you want to know the mic is on, tap it lightly. This won't damage it. Better yet, trust your system engineer to turn on the mic when it's needed.
- Speak with enough energy that the audience in the fifth row can hear you without a mic. Let the system engineer adjust levels from there.
- Check with your system engineer to be sure your wireless mic has fresh batteries.
- If the mic stops working or develops terrible noise interference, and it looks as if there will be no technical help, step away from the mic and speak up to be heard. The audience will appreciate your not giving up or becoming flustered.
- Always assume the mic is on. If you need to say something to someone in private, ask that the mic either be removed or turned off.

- Covering the mic with your hand does not protect what you say from being heard. Your somewhat muffled statement may be heard and come back to bite you.

- Don't turn the transmitter on or off before letting the sound engineer know, as this may result in a loud noise.

- If you are using a wireless mic, leave your cell phone or BlackBerry in a safe place away from you in the off mode. This will prevent embarrassing interference to your microphone.

- Keep a glass or cup of room temperature water nearby in case you need it during your presentation. Don't ice the water.[15] Anytime during your presentation, you can pause and take a sip. Remember, the audience wants you to be comfortable and successful. Don't over use the water glass as a prop or it will become distracting.

---

15 Ice water constricts the vocal chords and a cold bottle of water may drip condensation on you.

During dress rehearsal

Hopefully, you will have an opportunity to check the equipment (sound, computer, remote control, PowerPoint, etc) prior to presenting before an audience.

In a complete rehearsal, you will always want to test the mic before assuming the platform. The sound engineer will adjust the system to let you to stand without favoring the microphone. With a properly balanced sound system, you should be able to stand 18 inches from a lectern or standing mic and be heard by all.

When you test the mic, use words that start with P, B and T.[16]. If you hear a popping sound, you're too close to the mic.

During your presentation

- When you're on stage, talk in your normal "show" volume; there's no need to yell.
- A good speaking level will allow you to be heard in the fifth row without a microphone.
- Don't lean into it. Insist the sound engineer adjust the mic to let you stand up straight and not need to "eat" it like an ice cream cone.

---

16 These are called plosives. Examples such as "popcorn," "potato," "butter" "toaster" all have a rush of air from your mouth.

- Learn to ignore the mic as well as the lectern once you begin.
- If you applaud while on mic, do so quietly. The clapping noise, amplified by the sound system, is very distracting.

What type of microphone?

Speakers generally use four types of microphones:

- Lectern-mounted mics
- Mics that clip onto your lapel or shirt, attached to a battery pack clipped onto your belt or pants (also known as lavaliere mics)
- The "headset" mic: a tiny mic on a thin wire suspended from your ear, near your mouth
- A mic on a stand

Using lectern mics

The microphone is not the stick shift on a race car. It's a sophisticated piece of equipment. Playing with it or adjusting the mic when it's on may result in you not being heard. Often the resulting mic noise will give you a bad start to the presentation before you even say anything. When you see someone do this, remember: it is just another way to waste nervous energy.

Using clip-on lavaliere mics

Many speakers use a clip-on lavaliere mic, including every newscaster you see on TV.

A lavaliere mic is particularly useful if you want to step away from the lectern, because it eliminates that lectern "barrier" between you and the audience.

You have to think about where to put the battery pack. Most battery packs clip onto your belt or the top of your pants.

If you are wearing a dress without a belt, you will want to get the belt pack in time to put it somewhere inside your clothing, allowing it to be secure with the wire running to the mic.

The "headset" mic

The "headset" mic[17] is a very light, flesh-colored boom that hooks over an ear, placing the mic element an inch from your mouth. Everyone from singers to sportscasters and corporate presenters enjoy the freedom provided by this type of mic.

With a headset mic, you don't have to hide the cord inside a shirt or blouse. There is no clothing noise from a jacket, tie, or sweater rubbing against the mic.

Women prefer the headset mic because it gives them greater fashion freedom; they don't have to wear a button-front shirt to hold the lavaliere mic.

Though a headset mic might seem uncomfortable at first, any discomfort will go away when you focus on your message.

The presenters I coach usually have a sound engineer and an assistant who will help you rig the mic.

One very soft-spoken executive found that using a headset mic so impressed his audiences, he now travels with his own. Often he is the only one wearing this type of mic, and he always sounds better than those using other types of mics.

---

17 Countryman E6 is very popular.

Standing mic

The fourth and certainly simplest mic is a standing mic, with or without a cord. You can usually lift the mic off the stand to use it, but I suggest you set it and forget it. When a standing mic is properly set up, you can stand 18 inches away from the mic stand and forget it's even there once you start.

I show people how easy this is by asking them to stand at the mic with one arm by their side, bent at a 45-degree angle.

This is the ideal distance from this mic. You can stand there and gesture all you want without hitting the mic or worrying about any of the trouble associated with a wireless mic.

Typically a wireless mic rents for $125 to $180 per day. That is a large incremental cost when you can do the same thing with a $30 per day hard-wired standing mic on stage.

Microphone advice from a famous religious leader

With audiences in the tens of thousands, a certain world-famous preacher is one of the most accomplished, experienced, effective public speaker of our time.

Among many other speaking techniques he has mastered is the use of a lavaliere microphone:

- He always makes sure the lavaliere microphone is pinned on his right-side jacket lapel – not in the center of his shirt or tie. He then uses this placement to enhance his presentation.
- When he wants to speak with significant volume, he will place his left hand on the lectern and shout with emphasis. This technique gains the attention of the crowd while not overloading the sound system.
- On the other hand, when he wants to whisper to the audience, he can be seen placing his right hand on the lectern, forcing his mouth close to the lavaliere microphone. By so doing, his whispers can be heard loud enough to be effective.

Using a teleprompter

My greatest experiences using teleprompters happened when I was working with President Ronald Reagan. President Reagan could look over the script once and deliver a very convincing speech using a teleprompter.

There are two types of teleprompters:

- TV newscasters use an over-the-camera-lens prompter.
- Politicians use the "presidential" model with two pieces of glass astride a lectern. The glass reflects an image of a video monitor on the floor below. This image is controlled by an operator backstage.

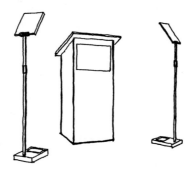

Using a teleprompter takes practice, starting with the way you format your prompter script. As I've advised earlier in this book, AVOID USING ALL CAPS ON TELEPROMPTER SCRIPTS. ALL CAPS ARE HARD TO READ.

Have the prompter operator insert stage directions in a different color or with special marks indicating DO NOT READ THESE INSTRUCTIONS. **<PAUSE FOR EMPHASIS>** is one of my favorite stage directions or reminders in a teleprompter script.

Make generous use of new paragraphs in a prompter script. Any trained operator will do this automatically.

Setting up the prompter

As with graphics monitors, teleprompter monitors on the floor near the stage should be placed as high off the floor as possible, so the audience doesn't see the top of your head every time you look down. Just as with a script on a lectern, practice your presentation so you can look down at the next thought and look up to deliver the message.

At TV awards shows, the teleprompter is on a big-screen TV 100 feet in the audience near the principal camera. That way it looks as if everyone is talking to the camera.

Corporate clients don't like this concept. They feel it gives away the teleprompter and distracts the audience.

In my experience, the audience will at first be intrigued by the prompters at the start of a well-rehearsed and meaningful presentation. Soon, however, they will focus on the stage, your message, and graphics.

You will always want to rehearse a teleprompter script out loud. For some strange reason, all the preparation in the world will always be tested by a live rehearsal. The operator will discover your pacing, phrasing, and speed. You will discover how to bring the message alive while seeming NOT to read.

Teleprompter tips

- Write your script to be read aloud, using your own words or phrases, to tell your stories.
- Rehearse, rehearse and rehearse. Make sure the same person is running the equipment during your rehearsal and speech.
- Ensure the prompter monitors are set off at such an angle that you can appear to be looking at your real audience while reading.
- Although there are two monitors, don't forget to talk to the audience between them. If you only look right and left, it will be further evidence you are reading.
- Keep a copy of the current script on the lectern or with someone off stage in case of equipment failure.

- If you keep a copy of the script on the lectern, have the prompter operator insert a symbol in the prompter (*) indicating page change. If you need the script, you will at least be on the right page.

Teleprompters are for a complete speech – NOT NOTES. A good prompter operator is like a pianist accompanying your singing. They move at your pace, not vice versa. Try it. If you speed up, so will the text in front of you. If you slow down, or pause, so will the script.

The operator can only see the few words displayed on the screen. If you use bullet points, or miss a point, the operator won't be able to "accompany" you. They will be lost until you return to the words on the screen.

Ad-libs when using teleprompter copy are dangerous. Insert **<AD LIB - story about the three horses walking into a bar>** then return to the script. The prompter operator will wait for you to tell your story, and then get back on script. You must return to the script right after the ad-libs. Otherwise, the operator will be lost, and you will be embarrassed.

Read the script as it rolls on the prompter. If it is good enough for the prompter, then read it that way. Don't challenge yourself and the operator by paraphrasing the message or juggling the words.

Dialogue with another presenter

It is often a good idea to include a second person for some or all of your presentation. This person could be a specialist, a typical audience member, or a colleague integral to the presentation.

When it is appropriate to use a second person, take the time to prepare and rehearse together. Agree on an outline together, and then write out the dialogue with clear points on who goes when. Each person needs to know their material and advance their own slides. **Don't memorize; have a conversation with each other.**

Look at each other when you begin talking. Then look at the audience, looking back occasionally to acknowledge your colleague is still interested. While your partner is speaking, don't let your mind and eyes wander. It's a signal to the audience they should do the same. Appear interested in what your partner is saying. React with head nods, or questions if appropriate.

When you are finished with your material, throw it to your partner by saying their name or asking a question while looking at them. When your partner begins to talk, facing the audience, you look at your partner.

Keep the dialogue simple. Keep the material conversational between the two of you.

If you are preparing from different cities, get together often on the phone to speak the parts. Do it often enough to coach each other and feel comfortable with the transitions.

Some sage advice: the night before

Common sense will tell you not to party all night before a big presentation. In my experience two people got caught up in the excitement of the pending meeting and partied until late the night before. One consultant was a hired gun with the planned "punctuation" for an important three-day meeting. His message was so important, he was the last person scheduled to speak on the last day. No such luck. He slept through his appointed time on stage…and lost the client.

The second experience was a recently promoted sales manager the night before the retirement party for his predecessor. There were so many "toasts" to his promotion, he slept through the announcement and prepared remarks celebrating the passing of the responsibilities. He didn't last long in that new job.

Get plenty of sleep. By the night before, if you've followed my advice from this book, you know the material well enough not to lose sleep worrying about the next day.

In the hours before your presentation, avoid drinking milk or milk by-products. They tend to create phlegm[18] that will be annoying to the audience and distracting to you.

Of course, don't go on stage with gum or a cough drop in your mouth.

Before going on stage, watch the previous presenter, not for content, but how are they doing? Are they making eye contact? How is their energy? What can you do to improve on that?

When you are invited to the stage, know your first line. Thank the person introducing you and connect with that person's message if you can. Shake that person's hand and keep them there for a moment.

> *Thanks Nancy, you made it very clear we need to follow the prescribed method to get the results we all strive for.*

Be specific. This will help dampen your jitters and give you, the previous speaker, and the audience the feeling that the message is on track and you intend to continue that trend.

---

18 The best lozenge I have found for throat problems before a speech is Fisherman's Friend.

I strongly differ with Ron Hoff[19] who wants you to think of the entire audience naked so you will have a feeling of power over them. I have tried to make a case in this brief time: you are in front of this audience for a reason. You must look at your peers, clients, or bosses as interested audience members engaged in your message. Respect them and treat them that way.

Beyond Bullet Points[20]

Cliff Atkinson is an independent consultant to leading attorneys and Fortune 500 companies. He designed the presentations that helped persuade a jury to award a $253 million verdict to the plaintiff in the nation's first Vioxx trial in 2005, which *Fortune* magazine called frighteningly powerful. Cliff's book, *Beyond Bullet Points,* expands on a communications approach he has taught at many of the country's top law firms, government agencies, business schools, and corporations.

I won't take the time to quote much of the book, but I will say Cliff Atkinson has shown great skill in improving the graphics side of a live presentation.

---

19 Ron Hoff is the author of I Can See You Naked: A Fearless Guide to Making Great Presentations, Andrews and McMeel, 1992.
20 Beyond Bullet Points by Cliff Atkinson, Microsoft Press, 2007.

In a recent online forum, Cliff gave this advice:

> *A major criticism of PowerPoint software is*
> *that it makes it too easy to do the wrong things,*
> *adding extraneous graphics and motion that*
> *quickly overwhelms. But we are where we are,*
> *and I don't see the software changing anytime*
> *soon, so we have to take the responsibility on*
> *ourselves to choose the few features that help*
> *us to align with the way the mind works,*
> *reduce overload, and increase the impact of our*
> *messages.*

If you Google "Death by PowerPoint" you will
find dozens of references on ways to improve your
graphics.

Is this too much on one slide?

- Create a paper copy of your most complex
  graphic.
- Place it on the floor.
- If you can read it standing up, use it.
- If not, don't.

As you prepare and practice for your presentation,
think about these other considerations and tools.

Screen size and placement

If you have the opportunity to influence the placement of the screen, pass along these tips.

- The screen must be large enough so properly prepared material is legible. The rule of thumb is that the viewer farthest away must be no further than eight times the height of the screen. If your audience is 64 feet from the screen, the screen must then be eight feet high.

- The screen bottom must be five feet up off the floor. Sit in the back row of your audience with people in the row ahead of you. If you have to look over any heads, you will not see anything lower than five feet in front of the room.

- Add it up. An eight-foot tall screen, positioned five feet above the floor represents a ceiling of at least 13 feet high. If you don't have a clear view (no chandeliers) from the back of the room, whatever is below five feet or on a screen smaller than eight feet high will be lost to the back rows.

Too many AV people, meeting planners, and trainers look at an empty room once everything is set up. They give approval while *standing* in the back of the room. That is not sufficient. Take the time to *sit in the back row*, preferably with people sitting in front of you. Then, adjust the screen and other AV equipment accordingly. Better yet, do the math ahead of time and have the equipment set up properly in the first place.

Exit stage right?

Stage directions were developed in the Greek theater. All stage directions are given from the actor vantage point. If you are to make a "stage right" exit, you are to walk to your right while facing the audience. Of course, "stage left" is the opposite way.

In the early days, the stage was elevated and slanted toward the audience. As a result, you are "up stage" if you are away from the audience. "Down stage" is closer to the audience.

PowerPoint 3-ups

When you are rehearsing in the mirror, use your 3-ups with notes. Speak out loud, with a tape recorder running. Your challenge is to look yourself in the eyes as often as possible. You will be able to transfer this skill to the stage.

Successful Q&A

Any opportunity to interact with the audience during your presentation adds to its value.

One interactive activity can be very successful: a Q&A period. Use Q&A at the beginning of your presentation to discover the audience's knowledge level. During your presentation, use Q&A to measure whether the audience is keeping up. At the end of your presentation, there is a great opportunity to cover issues you may not have touched with a Q&A session.

Don't use Q&A unless you are confident you know the answers to the questions likely to be asked. Prepare subject experts to assist you if an anticipated question presents a problem for you.

Most Q&A sessions begin with a planted question or two to let the audience know it is OK to ask questions. Before you begin, ask to have the house lights turned up full. You want to be able to recognize anyone with their hand up.

- Repeat the question (paraphrasing if necessary).
- Answer the question, or introduce someone else to answer the question or discuss, or commit to finding the answer within a reasonable time frame.
- Confirm your answer satisfied the questioner.

In a large room, clients often request a dozen mics for Q&A in an attempt to shorten the time between questions. This is false optimism and expensive.

Remember, only one person can question at a time. Having more than three wireless handheld mics in the audience is impractical and confusing to the presenter.

Wireless mics can be passed around. I prefer to have a "mic wrangler" available in the audience – someone who can encourage questions and coach the questioner to stand up and use the mic properly. The colleague should also assist you in finding the questioner in the audience. Always try to have the next questioner "cued up" to keep things moving along.

Some clients use a large sign with numbers representing the mic number (1, 2, or 3). The sign can be waved to the stage manager assisting the host, letting him or her see where the next questioner is available. The host should then recognize the next questioner with "I see we have a question at mic number 2." This also alerts the sound engineer to have that mic ready for the question.

Some Q&As use standing mics in the aisles. Depending on the seating density, however, a spontaneous discussion can be difficult when this configuration is used.

When Q&A time is up, someone must signal we have time for one more question," so as not to appear rude. That one question can also be planted with a trusted person.

Follow up your Q&A session with a quick summary if this is the end of your presentation. If you promised follow-up, do so promptly. And, if another speaker will follow you, be sure to introduce them.

The audience-polling technology tool

OptionPower® software and wireless keypads from Option Technologies[21] are a simple add-on to PowerPoint, allowing you to poll your audience for their input. This valuable software offers rock-solid technology that can be used in many different types of applications, from game shows to audience reaction to verifying audience understanding of a presentation.

---

21 Visit www.optiontechnologies.com for more information on audience-polling technology.

Once the software is loaded in your computer, audience question graphics can be created within PowerPoint asking their opinions or answers on any number of topics.

Answers can be anonymous so you get real reactions. Behind the software, you will also be able to create an Excel spreadsheet of all answers, sorted by any demographic.

I have used this audience-polling technology with a wide range of clients; every time, the audience responded favorably about using the keypads. More importantly, the clients were delighted at the wealth of information in the answers garnered from this technology.

Panel discussions

Often a misused tool for corporate meetings, the panel discussion has a good reason to exist. Decide very early whether a presentation will be a discussion with real interactivity or one-at-a-time speeches.

If you choose to have a panel discussion, select a moderator who has knowledge of the subject and clear objectives. The moderator should support each member of the panel.

Coach the panel members to be direct and brief if you are presenting the information from a 30,000-foot perspective. This also applies to your entire presentation. Remember the appropriate level for the audience's needs.

CONCLUSION

When you started reading this book, you were promised tools to help you make your next presentation a success.

I hope this is what you have learned.

- Know your audience.
- Prepare your material.
- Rehearse aloud.
- Speak with confidence to one person at a time.
- Use technology and techniques to your advantage.
- Sit down and take credit for accomplishing what you came to do and for doing so with skill and confidence.

Teaching these tools to a motivated participant

As I mentioned earlier, I have coached hundreds of middle managers and employees of Fortune 500 companies using the techniques described in this book. These methods have always been successful with anyone who had a message to deliver and a tight timeline in which to do so.

You, too, can teach these tools to your colleagues. In this book I occasionally repeated important points intentionally. The layout is intended to also be a useful reference book.

This is not a classroom activity. A small group of 10 or fewer is best.

Ideal candidates are nervous with a great motivation for success, just like you once were. Your job is to use that energy and a dose of empathy to keep them focused on the tools they need.

Very early in the process, I ask candidates to stand up, pretend the audience is ready and you are blocking the view. This simulates the real life stand-up practice everyone must go through. Explain the difference between mental and speaking processing speeds, and why simple distractions can torpedo the important moment.

Explain good practice technique. Send the candidate off to practice. Arrange a follow-up rehearsal with a feedback session where you provide them with notes for improvement.

It is very important to have a brief notes session following the actual meeting and presentation. The candidates will want to tell you how they feel about their newfound skills, and they will want your feedback as well.

Your impact will last a lifetime. These skills are very personal, owned differently by each person.

It is very gratifying to receive thank you notes as my clients are promoted, crediting their presentation skills as they learned these on-the-job public speaking tools.

Recently the Human Resources VP from a major corporate client announced to his staff how much my efforts have helped him. He related a very personal story on how he prepared for this brother's "Celebration of Life."

In the previous week, his dying brother had insisted the service be a family celebration, not a sad event. When the time came, this very influential corporate person reached into his memory of more than a dozen years for my coaching techniques.

The event went so well, his entire family applauded his tribute. "My brother would have been very proud," he told his staff.

Needless to say, this is high praise.

Give these tools to anyone faced with a similar situation and you, too, will understand the motivation that keeps me going.

And finally ...

How many times have you heard someone speak
to a large audience say "And finally..." then go
on for many more minutes before saying "In
conclusion..." often followed minutes later by "To
summarize..."

I will fight that urge. I suggest you do the same. I
will simply say ...

Thank you.

<WAIT FOR APPLAUSE>.

It is now time for a coffee break. <LOL>